Dozens of Ways to Make Money

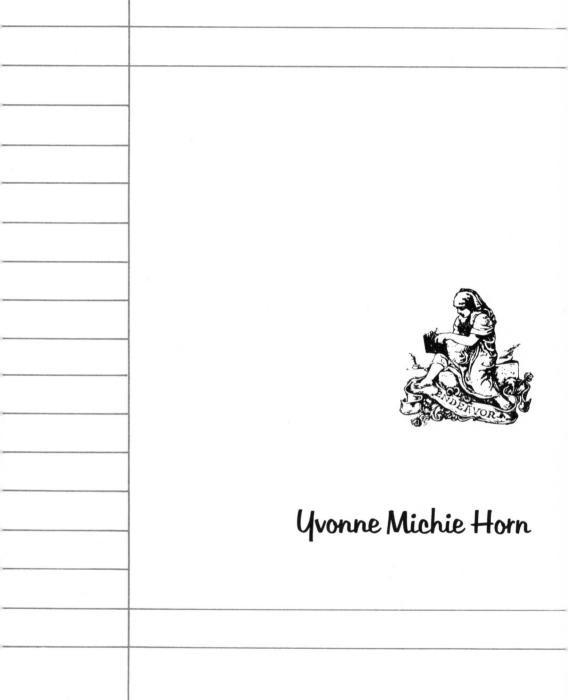

Yvonne Michie Horn

Dozens
of ways to
make money

Harcourt Brace Jovanovich

 New York and London

Printed in the United States of America

Library of Congress Cataloging in Publication Data

Horn, Yvonne Michie.
  Dozens of ways to make money.

    1. Vocational guidance. 2. Self-employed. 3. Stu-
dent employment. I. Title.
HF5381.H64   331.7′02   76–39930
ISBN 0–15–224184–1
ISBN 0–15–224185–X pbk.

First edition

B C D E F G H I J K

To my grandfather, WILLIE MICHIE,
who always asked,
"How much for cash?"

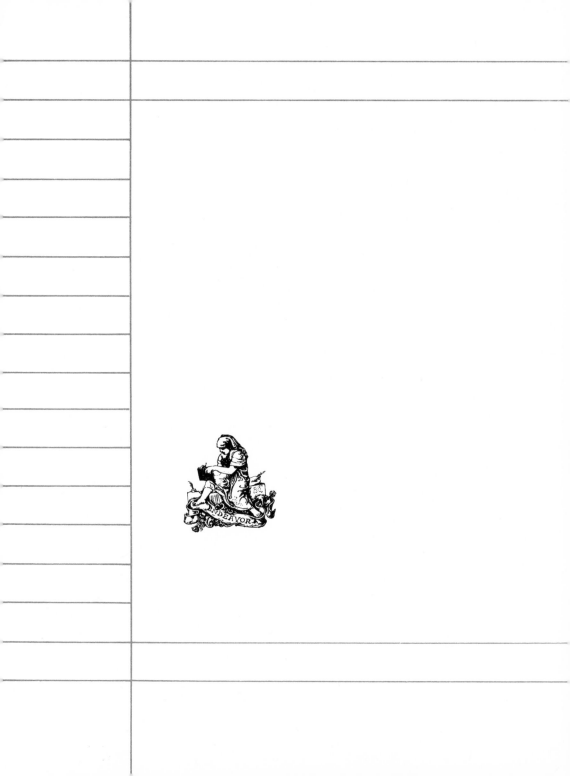

Contents

87857

Author's Note

Hundreds of young entrepreneurs contributed to *Dozens of Ways to Make Money*. They live in all parts of the country, in towns big and small. What they have in common is job imagination . . . the ability to turn a unique idea into cash.

These young entrepreneurs shared their ideas with me. Some responded through a questionnaire sent to high schools from Maine to California, a questionnaire that asked, "Do you make money from a job you thought up yourself?" Others came to my attention when their activities were featured in newspaper accounts. Still others made the book by word of mouth: "You should talk to so-and-so—she has the best idea and it's making money!"

All of the people written about are real. Most are called by their true names; others asked that their identities be changed. In some of the ways to make money, several reported doing the same thing. They are written about as a composite person with the best taken from each operation.

It was impossible to cite exact cost figures for initial supplies in every instance. In any case costs would vary from state to state. Sometimes the entrepreneurs already had some of the necessary supplies on hand before embarking on their money-making projects.

It is unlikely that other young people who wish to become entrepreneurs would want to duplicate in exact detail the jobs described in this book, but I hope they will be inspired to use their own imagination and creativity to develop their own special ways of making money. Also, for some of the jobs described in this book, questions may arise in regard to insurance, licenses, certificates, etc., and advice should be sought from people knowledgeable in these areas.

My mailbox was never dull during the writing of *Dozens of Ways to Make Money.* Ingenious, funny, optimistic . . . every letter from a job inventor proved that there's nothing more amazing than people.

Y.M.H.

Dozens of Ways to Make Money

The Boss Is You

Jobs are hard to find. Anyone who's tried to land part-time or after-school work will tell you that. But even so, you can fill your pockets with spending money and have enough left over to salt away in a rainy-day bank account. Here's the way to do it.

Be your own boss. Think up your own work to do. Hundreds of teen-agers across the country have found that this is the one sure way to beat the "Sorry! No help needed" blues.

So, stop reading the help-wanted ads. Stop fussing over that application with its long spaces asking you to list the previous experience you don't have. Stop worrying about whether or not you'll be able to work the hours demanded and stay awake in class too. Become one of the self-employed. This book lists thirty-six ways teen-agers, in the same boat as you, have done just that.

They've found that when you're the boss you can capitalize on your own special interests, talents, and abilities. You can juggle your work schedule around the demands of school and family. What's more, when the time comes that you're faced with those empty "previous work experience" spaces, you'll be able to fill them in.

You have lots of freedom when you're the boss. But those who've been successful in their own businesses know that freedom is a two-way street. Sure, there's no one standing over you threatening instant dismissal if you don't produce. Instead, you stand over you. Can you discipline yourself to do your best all on your own? An honest affirmative answer is crucial to success. Of course you answered "yes." So, read on.

Anyone who buys your time has every right to expect you to be on the beam the entire hour, half-day, or whatever you promised. If you're tutoring Susie in math from 4:30 to 5:30 every Wednesday afternoon, Susie's parents have a right to be annoyed if you arrive at 4:31 and then take three minutes out for a phone call. Four minutes short may not seem much to you, but they've bought sixty, not fifty-six, minutes of your time. Always give full measure—and, occasionally, a dividend of a bit more.

The idea of giving a bit more extends to quality too. If you're making something for sale, it must be as good or better than that which can be bought at a store. You can probably count on Uncle Willard to buy one of your rumpled, homemade neckties, and even wear it once, because you're his favorite niece. That nice lady next door will undoubtedly shell out for a box of your "special," somewhat stale, caramel corn just to be kind. You may sell a few bunches of yesterday's wilted carrots and radishes to a neighbor who hates to say no. But you can bet that even Uncle Willard and the kind neighbors won't help you out more than once. Strangers won't buy at all.

Which brings us to a word about advertising. There are many ways to let people know you're in business: announcements pinned on neighborhood bulletin boards, posters in store windows, ads in the local papers, fliers delivered door to door. But word of mouth is the most valuable advertising of all. And that you cannot buy or print up to tack on a wall. Word-of-mouth advertising depends solely on your reputation to deliver exactly what you promised.

O.K., you're willing to walk the extra mile, and you're convinced that what you have to offer is of top-notch quality. There's still another consideration before you set up shop.

Who needs it? You won't sell many yard-long woolly mufflers if you live in Miami. It's doubtful if too many big-city apartment dwellers will subscribe to your snow-shoveling service. And you won't have too much luck with a roadside flower stand if you live on a Nevada cattle ranch. Exaggerated? Of course. But many good ideas fall short simply because their creator failed to offer what his neighbors needed.

Find a need and fill it; that's the prime consideration. Put on your thinking cap and brainstorm the question: What does my locality need that I can provide? Be creative in your thinking. Remember that your prospective customers may not realize they need your service until you tell them. For instance, in Flagstaff, Arizona, a neighborhood made up of retired people who liked to travel didn't know they needed someone to take care of their indoor greenery while they were away. Today they have a very busy "plant sitter" who regularly visits the bank. Homeowners in Sacramento, California, found a new sense of community spirit when Pete Hollenbeck's *Wilhaggin Times* rolled off his Mimeograph. This informal weekly paper is now in its tenth year and is still going strong with its theme of neighborliness. Perhaps you live in a rural area where "putting up" produce is part of the summer chores. One girl in southern Oregon advertised herself as a Canner's Helper and "put up" enough money to finance new skiing equipment and a winter of fun on the slopes.

Whatever job you create, be businesslike. Keep an appointment book so you won't get crossed up on the wheres and whens of your operation. Give out receipts and keep a copy. In a ledger keep track of what you've spent for supplies. Write down who paid you and how much. It's the only way to be certain you're making money. It will also guide you in improving your operation so you can make even more.

Part of being businesslike is making certain that you're operating within the letter of the law. Always check to be sure whether you need to purchase insurance, licenses, or certificates for any of your money-making projects. The zoning commission will undoubtedly frown if you are raising guinea hens on your apartment-house balcony. The Food and Drug Administration might like to take a good look at your secret recipe for pickled beans. And the Internal Revenue Service will be most interested in an accounting of your earnings.

Another side of businesslike behavior is to price yourself or your product realistically. Too often, beginning business people, anxious to make the sale at any price, charge much less than the service or article is worth. So there you are with a contract to prune an acre of apples for a fee that barely buys the gasoline to get you there. Long before the job is finished, you will probably find yourself seething with resentment as you hack away at the branches. Chances are you won't do as good a job as when fairly paid. Neither you nor the fellow who got you for the bargain rate will be happy.

So learn to estimate the number of hours a job will take. Price your time at the going rate. If you're making an item to sell, figure in the cost of supplies and give yourself a fair salary for creation time. Check around to see what similar articles are selling for. Price accordingly. If you can't realistically compete, think up a new idea.

Begin small. Buy only the supplies you need. Advertise only to the number of customers you can easily handle. A modest success you can grow on is far better than a grandiose flop.

Give your business a name. It gives your prospective customers a feeling of permanence and reliability if they know they are dealing with something that has a title. Be clever, if you like, but not so obscurely clever that the people you hope to deal with have no idea what you do or sell. "The Far Out Orange Onion" will leave your prospective customers scratching their heads. "The Auto Laundry" makes it perfectly clear that you wash cars for a living.

If you can afford it, have some business cards printed up. If not, hand-letter your own, perhaps on heavy construction paper. Not only do cards identify you immediately, but they also give your contacts something to hang on to should they want to give you a call later. And, again, a card implies reliability and a businesslike attitude. Chances are you'll get the order if you present your card—"The Great Grate Filler," Wood to Burn, Jack Jones, Phone 369-4210—as you give your door-to-door pitch. Guess what the answer will be if you ring the bell, shuffle your feet, and ask, "Need some wood?"

A businesslike attitude and reliability coupled with a top-notch idea spell success. But what if, despite your efforts, the world's not ready for your spectacular idea? So what! Think up another moneymaker. You have dozens more stored away in your head. In fact, that's the purpose of this book, to get your job-inventing imagination in high gear. The next six chapters will help you on your way by describing what others like you have done to fill their pockets with cash.

So, unleash your creativity. Take stock of your unique talents, interests, and abilities. You have all the qualifications and know-how to be a success. Ready, set, go . . . there's money ahead.

2

You Can Earn Dollars from Discards

"One guy's trash is another fellow's treasure" might well be the motto of the many teen-aged job inventors who are cleaning up on throwaways. In their eyes, junk is not mere junk. Refurbished, recycled, turned into something not remotely resembling their garbage-can origins, discards mean dollars.

You'll find many advantages to a business based on discards. For one, ecologically speaking, you're reusing materials. Also, you're in a position to help out your friends, relatives, and neighbors . . . people are always delighted to have their no-longer-wanteds hauled away. But the biggest advantage of all is that your basic materials are absolutely free.

Here are six ideas that will help you get started poking around in attics and trash barrels, in fields and beaches. All of these tried-and-true "throwaway" businesses make money. Yours can too!

WEEDS FOR SALE

Common, ordinary, troublesome weeds—that's what Tim, "The Weedman," turns into money. But by the time Tim dries, bunches, and packages his roadside pickings, those undesirable weeds are "decorative grasses," much in demand for today's natural-looking bouquets.

Advertising: Tim visits flower shops, boutiques, variety stores, decorating studios, and businesses, such as banks, which use permanent floral displays. He introduces himself as "The Weedman" and shows samples of his bundles of mixed grasses. Tim is prepared to take orders on the spot and always leaves his business card —an attractive, straw-colored rectangle of heavy construction paper hand-lettered in brown ink.

Initial Supplies: Business cards, cellophane bags, drying chemicals, string and cord, lumber for shelves and a work table.

Method of Operation: Tim visited the library and read up on the art of drying flowers. Then he set up shop in a corner of the family garage. He built shelves and a long work table, and arranged hanging areas for drying.

"I'm constantly on the watch for fields of different

types of weeds—lace grass, Scotch broom, cattails, wheat, statice, straw flowers," Tim says. At the height of the grass season, late summer, most of Tim's time is spent collecting enough material to keep The Weedman in business through the winter.

When the grasses are dry, Tim selects the weeds according to each customer's order—mixed, all one type, long-stemmed, short—and packages them in a cellophane bag secured with brown cord. He ties a business card on each order. Prices range from 75 cents for a small bunch of ordinary grasses up to $10 for a large assortment of unusual varieties.

Tim puts in about twelve hours a week during the school year and at least twice that during the summer months. According to the season—fall and winter are the most popular months for dried grasses—Tim's income ranges from $100 to $500 a month.

Tim's Comments: "My next step is to get into pre-arranged bouquets . . . you know, in a basket with a gingham bow, that sort of thing. As gift items for special days, they should sell well."

PAGLUCCI AND MORETTI, PRODUCE

A junked 1932 Ford produce truck helped Sam become a moneymaker. Authentically restored and sporting a yellow and green striped awning, it's a welcome sight on the residential streets of Sam's town. Housewives appreciate his farm-fresh vegetables. And Sam's old-time hanging scales and brown paper bags make the picking out of tomatoes and corn more fun than shopping at a supermarket. Why does he call his business Paglucci and Moretti? "It had a nice Italian vegetable-vendor ring that I liked," says Sam. "Neither is my name."

Advertising: Sam's truck is his best advertisement. He drives his traveling market slowly down the streets, discreetly honking his horn to let his customers know he's on their block. When someone runs out to buy, he reminds them that he will be in their neighborhood at the same time the following week. Frequently, shoppers ask that he make a weekly stop in front of their house. Sam lists their addresses in a notebook. He also offers to special-order any out-of-the-ordinary fruit or vegetables that he may not carry routinely on his truck.

Initial Supplies: Outfitted truck, paper bags, $25 to buy produce on the first day of operation.

Method of Operation: Paglucci and Moretti, Produce is a summertime job for Sam. Early each morning he visits the wholesale vegetable market in his town and chooses only the best of the produce offered. He loads the boxes on the slanting sides of his truck, fills a watering can with ice water to sprinkle over the more perishable items as he goes along, and prices his produce with tags. "I always check the newspaper ads to keep in line with what the supermarkets are charging," he says. Sam is ready for business. On an average day, Paglucci and Moretti, Produce clears $50.

Sam's Comments: "The hardest thing to learn was how much to buy. That came with hard experience. Wilted, leftover vegetables become costly garbage when you're in the fresh produce business. Now that Paglucci and Moretti is going well, it's a great way to make my love of old vehicles pay for itself."

LEAF MOLD MAKER

Leaves in Larry's tree-shaded town were either bundled up for the garbage man to haul away or swept up and dumped by municipal sweeping crews. Then Larry came along, and although he hasn't been able to recycle all of his city's leaves, he's made a big dent in some of the piles. Bagged, composted, and sold, Larry's organic leaf mold makes his neighbors' gardens, and his bankbook, grow.

Advertising: Larry posted notices on neighborhood bulletin boards. He also asked hardware-store owners to tape his fliers near their cash registers and contacted garden clubs in his area.

Initial Supplies: Large, heavy-duty plastic garbage bags. Shovel, ammonium sulfate, labels, leaves.

Method of Operation: His first autumn in business, Larry asked neighbors for their leaves. "I felt kind of silly," Larry says, "like I was too poor to have my own." The next fall, he expanded his composting operation and asked the street sweepers to dump leaves in his driveway.

Larry sprinkles down the leaves as they arrive and lets them sit in the weather until they are limp and soggy. Then he begins to shovel. He stuffs each plastic sack tight with leaves, sprinkles in a handful of ammonium sulfate—"It speeds up breakdown and adds nitrogen," Larry explains—ties up the sack, and puts it aside to let Mother Nature do her composting work. The plastic bag helps generate heat and hurries up the process.

By spring, when gardeners are beginning to think about tilling their soil, Larry's compost is ready for use. He glues a label on each sack that reads "Organic Compost, Pure Leaf Mold," and sells it for $1.50 a bag. He agrees to deliver, free of charge, orders of ten sacks or more.

Plastic bags cost Larry 8 cents apiece, the ammonium sulfate is thrown in for 2 cents a handful, labels are 10 cents each, but the main ingredient is free. Profit on each sack, $1.30. Larry fills 500 sacks each fall.

Larry's Comments: "Five hundred sacks piled up is an overwhelming sight. My mother is sure glad when spring comes."

GARAGE SALE

Twice a year Jennifer and Sue gather up no-longer-wanteds and put on a sale in Sue's garage. Neighbors, friends, and relatives clean out their sheds and closets and add to the girls' accumulation of dollar-making discards. "It's a good arrangement," says Sue. "We clean up and they clean out!"

Advertising: Sue's house is on a well-traveled suburban street. The girls post signs at nearby cross streets and in front of Sue's house.

Initial Supplies: Pins, small squares of paper, and grease pencils for marking prices. Hangers, rope, card tables, notebook, change.

Method of Operation: Two days before the sale, Sue and Jennifer unpack their six-month accumulation of salables in Sue's garage. They mark sizes and prices, press clothing, and hang garments on rope strung across the garage. Other items are put in categories—household goods, sports equipment, tools—and shined up to look as attractive as possible.

On sale days, the friends take turns manning the garage. "We find that people don't want to be helped," says Sue. "We sell more if we just let them browse." "But we do post a sign, 'Haggle Spoken Here,'" adds Jennifer.

Some large items are sold on consignment. "For instance, we kept 20 percent for selling a sewing machine for my aunt," Jennifer explains. The two friends keep track of consignment sales in their notebook. "With the rest of the stuff, Jennifer and I simply split the profits," Sue says, "no matter who brought what. And we usually clear around $300 each."

Anything not sold by five o'clock Sunday is packed away for the next sale. "Someone, sometime will buy it," says Jennifer.

Sue's and Jennifer's Comments: "We've found, especially with clothing that has a prestigious label, that if it hasn't sold on Saturday, mark it up, not down. People seem to think if they pay more, it must be better!"

DRIFTWOOD STEPPING STONES

The raw materials for Bob's business regularly appear with the ocean tide. Runaway trees from California's north coast lumber mills litter the beaches near his house—driftwood free for the hauling.

Cut into rounds, the abandoned logs become stepping stones, much in demand for California's casual gardens.

Initial Supplies: Truck, electric table saw.

Advertising: Bob does no written advertising. Instead, he visits garden-supply and discount stores and talks to landscape designers and gardeners. He offers to take orders on the spot and always leaves his telephone number so that he can be contacted easily.

Method of Operation: Bob's four-wheel-drive truck is equipped with a winch. Every few weeks he drives out to the beach and picks out the best of the logs, hoists them out of the sand, and hauls them home. Then he cuts the wood into three-inch-thick rounds—"You'd be surprised how many step-stones can be cut from one washed-up tree," Bob says—ties them with baling wire into bundles of six, loads them on his truck, and delivers his wooden stones to his customers. Bob charges $3.50 a bundle and sells an average of eighteen bundles each Saturday for a $63 profit.

Bob's Comments: "I used to worry that I'd strip the beaches bare and work myself out of business. But that just doesn't happen. Every storm and high tide brings me a whole new supply."

THE RECYCLED LOGGER

When Eileen began to roll up newspapers, the money started rolling in too. Her 4½-inch-thick, 20-inch-long newspaper "logs" are burning in fireplaces all over town.

Advertising: Eileen borrows her little brother's high-sided wooden wagon when she goes out to sell her logs door to door. On each side of the wagon she hangs a sign that lists the advantages of the Recycled Logger's product: long-burning, colorful, ecologically sound, inexpensive, termite-free. As the Christmas holidays near, Eileen adapts her signs to the season and advertises her newspaper rolls as Yule logs.

To encourage her customers to reorder, each log is stamped "The Recycled Logger. Call: 707-5673."

Initial Supplies: Twine, detergent, large tub, color crystals, wood-patterned paper, rubber stamp, log-rolling machine, newspapers.

Method of Operation: Eileen's big expense was her sturdy log roller, bought from a mail-order house for $18. The cost of the rest of her supplies tallies up to less than 10 cents a log.

Most of the log-rolling work is done in the summer. "I soak the rolled and tied newspapers in water that has a little detergent thrown in," she explains. "Then I dry the soggy logs in the sun until they are hard as wood. It helps if it's hot outside."

Eileen sprinkles color crystals, bought at a fireplace shop, on the center newspaper before she runs it through her log-making machine. Soaking distributes the color throughout the roll. "The logs burn with a rainbow of flames," Eileen says.

Each dried log is then wrapped in wood-patterned paper (bought at a wallpaper store), rubber-stamped "The Recycled Logger," and tied into bundles of three.

When the weather turns cool, Eileen loads up her

wagon and hits the streets. She prices her logs at three for 75 cents.

Eileen's Comments: "To show you how great my newspaper logs are, my parents no longer have firewood delivered. Instead, they order exclusively from The Recycled Logger."

You Can Turn Fun into Funds

3

Make a list of the ten activities you enjoy the most. Lucky you, at least five on that list may be money-makers. There's funds to be made from fun.

Those teen-agers who play for pay report that their work is far from bone-tiring and dreary. Often, it's the high point of their day. What's more, they've found that when you like what you do, your enthusiasm shines through and adds immeasurably to success.

So turn your job-inventing attention to your special interest, talent, or hobby. Then expand it, twist it around, turn it inside out until it becomes something you can share, teach, or sell to others. With a business based on pleasure, you'll hardly be able to wait to go to work!

A MONSTER FOR ALL SEASONS

When Glenn appeared at a Halloween costume party dressed as an eight-foot-tall version of himself, it was just for fun. He was still having fun when he added a mask and began to show up at more parties, not as a guest but by request. It was then that moneymaking possibilities began to flicker through Glenn's head. He improved his costume, printed up cards, and the business he calls Frankenstein came into being.

Advertising: Glenn's business is built almost entirely on word-of-mouth advertising. Those who see him as the enormously tall, realistic-looking Frankenstein are quick to tell others. But to help pass the word along, Glenn dresses up now and then and takes a leisurely stroll around town. He hands out business cards as he goes.

Initial Supplies: Stilts, black suit, mask, horrible hands.

Method of Operation: Frankenstein hires himself out for children's parties, adult gatherings, community events, and business promotions. His basic charge is $25 an appearance, or $25 an hour. When Frankenstein appears at a party, he stays only fifteen or twenty minutes. "I leave before the fright impact wears off," Glenn explains. For other events, such as an opening of a shopping center, Frankenstein's contract calls for a minimum stay of two hours, which nets him at least $50 for the appearance.

To extend Frankenstein's popularity for more than the traditional October "scaring" month, Glenn added simple accessories to his basic black suit to create a monster for all seasons. At Thanksgiving, Frankenstein wears a pilgrim's hat and fresh white cuffs. Christmastime sees him in a beard and red cap with a pillow stuffed under his belted jacket. At Easter, Frankenstein pins on pink and white floppy ears and carries a frilly basket filled with colored eggs.

Glenn's Comments: "My friends thought I was nuts when I spent $80 on a professional Frankenstein mask and hands—my only big expense, by the way. I've been playing Frankenstein for two and a half years now. That $80 was the best investment I ever made."

RAFT PARTIES

Jeff, Mark, Mike, and Marc plan parties for a price. RAFT stands for Rio Americano (the name of their high school) Fun Times. But their name also came about because float trips are a RAFT specialty. Whether it's a barbecue, a day on the river, a picnic in the park, or a dinner dance and amateur show, the four Rafters have a ball with their business.

Advertising: The four Rafters mimeograph promotional fliers and stick them in their friends' lockers at school.

Initial Supplies: None.

Method of Operation: The Rafters' first party was a Memorial Day raft trip on the river that runs through their town. Twenty-five people paid $2 each to go floating. Partygoers brought their own rafts and picnic lunches; the Rafters provided cold drinks. A $10 prize went to the fastest rafter down the river.

A barbecue netted the Rafters $120. They bought the meat at the rate of 75 cents for three big beef ribs and sold the meaty-monsters for 75 cents a single rib.

One hundred friends bought tickets at $5 each to come to a prime rib dinner and show. The catered dinner cost the Rafters $2 a plate. The management of the hired hall charged them 75 cents a person. Show-time entertainment was provided by talented friends from school.

The Rafters' Comments: "Our parties are successful because the four of us work well together. And we keep things simple: lay out a plan, decide who does what, have a good time, and then go put our money in the bank."

THE GREAT GIUSEPPE

Joe can't remember a time when he wasn't pulling twelve yards of silk cloth out of his sleeve or asking someone to choose a card, any card, from a freshly shuffled deck. But it was only when Joe decided to spread his magical talent around that gold began to appear in his pockets.

Advertising: Joe pins up cards in Laundromats, in grocery stores, on neighborhood bulletin boards: "The Great Giuseppe, Children's Parties a Specialty, Magic Shows by a Very Professional Young Man."

The Great Giuseppe is also listed under Magicians in the yellow pages of the telephone directory.

Initial Supplies: Basic magic equipment.

Method of Operation: Joe's business actually began  years before his first paying show. His parents gave him a beginner's magic kit for his birthday. Boom! He was hooked.

Joe read every book on magic that he could get his hands on and asked his librarian to order more. "Magicians are self-taught," he says. "Few magicians will share their tricks."

Joe looked in the yellow pages of his telephone book and found there was a magician's supply store in his town. He began to accumulate the equipment needed to do the tricks described in the books he read. And then he practiced, practiced, practiced. "You've got to be good if

you're going to ask people to shell out money to watch," Joe says.

He charges $15 for a half-hour performance at a child's party. Some months are busier than others, but over a year's time he averages one show a week. "That gives me more than enough money to keep my saws sharp enough to cut people in half," the Great Giuseppe says.

Joe's Comments: "The psychological aspects of magic are fascinating. What makes people overlook what you don't want them to see? But most of all, magic is fun. And if an audience has fun with you, they're going to ask you back to do another show."

UMPIRE

Rich can't remember a time when he wasn't playing on one team or another. Sports are the love of his life. Too, Rich's father professionally umpired minor-league ball games twenty-five years ago. So it was only natural for Rich to look for pay dirt on his city's diamonds.

A true professional, Rich "umps" all over town, not only for baseball, but basketball and football games too.

Advertising: Rich contacts his city and county recreation departments, schools, Little Leagues, and adult sport leagues. He introduces himself as a professional member of his local officials' association, presents his card, and outlines his umpiring experience.

Initial Supplies: Mask, chest protector, left-hand indicator, shin guards, dark pants, striped shirt, coaches' shoes.

Method of Operation: "An umpire has to know more than the rules of the game," Rich says. "He also must know the mechanics of umpiring—the correct signals, how to position himself on the field." To learn the mechanics, Rich joined his local association of umpires, paid the $10 membership fee, and attended the free clinics offered by the professional group.

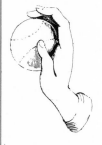

"Uniforms are the biggest expense," says Rich. "Around $125 to be completely outfitted, unless you're lucky enough to buy used equipment. Shin guards, masks . . . all of that stuff really adds up." Rich's basketball and football uniforms—dark pants, powder-blue shirt—were put together from his own wardrobe. "But I did have to buy the traditional striped 'ump's shirt,'" Rich adds.

Rich notes upcoming games in his date book. "Then all I do is show up and do my job," he says. A Little League game pays him $7, adult games $15, with another $10 to $15 added on for a doubleheader.

Rich's Comments: "Baseball is the most dangerous to umpire. Last season I had my mask raised to check third base when the kid at bat struck out, got mad, and threw his bat. Wham! Right in the mouth!"

27

87857

EMPEROR NORTON'S IMPERIAL ORCHESTRA

Rob fiddles away his time on street corners—and gets paid for doing it. Along with two or three or four friends —depending on who can come—Rob's cello, a viola, two violins, and a French horn make up one of San Francisco's finest street-musician quintets, quartets, or trios. They call themselves Emperor Norton's Imperial Orchestra.

Says Rob, "For anyone thinking of doing a public gig, like street playing, it's a good angle to choose a name that is identifiable with city lore. Emperor Norton, for example, was an ex-millionaire turned lovable beggar. Everyone who knew about the Emperor loved him, so it is easier for them to like us . . . and hand us their money."

Advertising: The musicians leave business cards and fliers in an easy-to-reach place while they play. Listeners pick them up and frequently call to arrange for special appearances.

Initial Supplies: Instruments and talented musicians.

Method of Operation: The Imperial musicians staked out a claim in front of a busy downtown bookstore. "Street players have a polite, unwritten rule that whoever gets a corner first has it," says Rob.

The musicians meet on their corner, set up music stands, and begin to play. Soon the corner is crowded with passersby stopping to listen to the professionally performed classical music. "We keep an instrument case open so they get the idea that's the place to drop in money," Rob says. Merchants are happy to have popular street musicians, like the Emperor Norton's, set up business in front of their stores. "We play well and bring in customers," Rob explains.

Mid-November through New Year's is the most lucrative season for street musicians. The summer tourist season runs a close second. Imperial Orchestra members can count on $7 an hour per player. Music time generally begins at 11:30, to take advantage of lunchtime crowds, and continues for two hours. They meet again around 4:30 and fiddle the downtown workers home.

Special parties pay $100 to $150. "Once we costumed ourselves in Victorian garb and played Strauss waltzes for an ice-skating party," Rob says. Another time, they appeared in formal dress and performed for a bank's meeting of stockholders.

Rob's Comments: "It really gets cold out there on that corner. I play my cello wearing mittens with the fingers cut out."

LESLIE PAINTS THE TOWN

Leslie's artwork is all over town—in store windows and on store windows. And some of her work is even delivered door to door with the daily newspaper. Leslie is a commercial artist who is lucky enough to earn her spending money doing what she likes to do best.

Advertising: Leslie visits small businesses. She presents her card, shows the owner a portfolio of photographs of her work, and offers her sign-painting and artistic services.

Initial Supplies: Poster board, poster paints, brushes.

Method of Operation: "Most of my signs are of the 'Order Your Thanksgiving Pies Early' and 'We Open at 9 A.M.' variety," Leslie says. But often she gets to paint a store's entire display window. "A candy store, for instance, has me design Halloween, Christmas, Easter—seasonal promotional scenes—for their window," she says.

On weekends Leslie works for another free-lance artist who does layouts for grocery-store ads in the newspaper. Leslie's total weekly work load is about twenty hours.

Leslie charges a minimum of $25 for a poster-painted storefront window. For signs and newspaper layouts she is paid $2.50 an hour.

Leslie's Comments: "Unlike other art, commercial work is here today, gone tomorrow. The season ends and my picture is gone forever, washed off with a hose and run down the gutter."

You Can Do the Dirty Work for Dollars

4

No one really gets a kick out of boring, messy, muscle-wearying chores. But if you're willing to take on one of the awful jobs no one else wants to do, you're almost guaranteed to earn as much money as you have hours to fill.

Write down all the duties you've heard people complain about: putting the garage in order, cleaning the oven, preparing house gutters for winter. . . . The list goes on and on.

Then pick out the one you think you can stand the best and put yourself in business. It helps as you go about your dirty work to keep whispering to yourself, "Look, I hate to do this, but oh, how I like those dollars!"

THE PARTY'S OVER

"How I hate to face those piles of dirty dishes!" That was Sally's mother's lament time and time again after an enjoyable evening entertaining guests. Sally figured other hostesses must feel the same way. She was right. The Party's Over has as much business as Sally can handle.

Advertising: Sally pins up her hand-printed business cards on neighborhood bulletin boards. She also advertises in every paper that doesn't charge for a listing, such as school newsletters and her church bulletin.

At every job, Sally leaves a few cards and suggests that the hostess tell her friends about the service.

Initial Supplies: Apron.

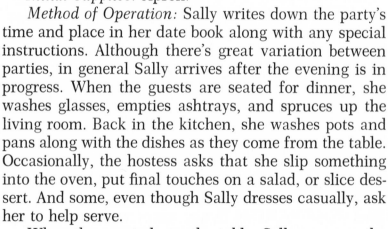

Method of Operation: Sally writes down the party's time and place in her date book along with any special instructions. Although there's great variation between parties, in general Sally arrives after the evening is in progress. When the guests are seated for dinner, she washes glasses, empties ashtrays, and spruces up the living room. Back in the kitchen, she washes pots and pans along with the dishes as they come from the table. Occasionally, the hostess asks that she slip something into the oven, put final touches on a salad, or slice dessert. And some, even though Sally dresses casually, ask her to help serve.

When the guests leave the table, Sally removes the

last dishes, blows out the candles, and takes off the cloth. She leaves when everything is shipshape.

Sally's basic charge is $2 an hour. Serving is 50 cents an hour extra, and if there are children to be fed and bedded, her price escalates to $3.

Sally's Comments: "I love parties, even when I'm behind the scenes. And, by the way, my mother is my best customer."

CLEANING UP AT THE TRACK

"With all those horses, they must need a shoveler," thought Tom. So he walked into the business office at the racetrack in his town and offered to do the job. He was hired on the spot.

Advertising: Tom doesn't advertise his service. "One racetrack is enough," he says. "Besides, it's the only one in town."

Initial Supplies: None. "They supply the shovel."

Method of Operation: Tom's job is to make sure the track area is free of manure before starting time. His duties are simple. "Shovel it up and dump it out," Tom explains.

Tom works seven hours a week during the racing season and is paid $7 an hour.

Tom's Comments: "What can I say? It's a job."

RICH'S GARDENING SERVICE

At the height of his career, Rich pruned, sprayed, and mowed for thirty-six customers and raked in $500 a month. And when his gardening days ended at the start of college, he sold his customer goodwill to a new backyard entrepreneur for $460. His truck brought him $650 more.

Advertising: "Although I have business cards, I never really advertised," Rich says. "It was mostly a matter of neighbors leaning over hedges and asking me to take a look at their yards. The business grew naturally, like a weed."

Initial Supplies: Basic gardening equipment.

Method of Operation: Rich inherited his first three customers from his brother. He used his family's equipment. When he accumulated enough money, he bought a truck and expanded to yards beyond his neighborhood.

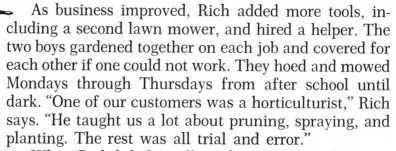

As business improved, Rich added more tools, including a second lawn mower, and hired a helper. The two boys gardened together on each job and covered for each other if one could not work. They hoed and mowed Mondays through Thursdays from after school until dark. "One of our customers was a horticulturist," Rich says. "He taught us a lot about pruning, spraying, and planting. The rest was all trial and error."

When Rich left for college, his gardening business

had not only provided him with ample spending money for his high school years, but he also had $4,000 in the bank.

Rich's Comments: "Sometimes out there in the hot summer sun I'd have to keep saying, 'It's good money, it's good money, it's good money.'"

LET THE SUN SHINE IN

When Jack appears with his ladder, squeegee, and bucket, homeowners know the sun will soon be shining in, for sparkling, streak-free windows are Jack's specialty. The business he calls Let the Sun Shine In keeps him as busy as he cares to be.

Advertising: Jack's business cards are printed on bright yellow paper. The card features a smiling sun peering through a windowpane. He leaves his card when he goes on doorbell-ringing expeditions and, hoping for repeat business, when he finishes a job. He also posts cards on community bulletin boards.

Initial Supplies: Ladder, squeegee, rags, bucket, commercial cleaning solution.

Method of Operation: Jack offers free estimates. On a pad of paper he writes down the amount to be charged and presents it to the customer along with his card. He keeps a carbon for his records. In general, he figures on $1.50 a window for inside and outside washing. The removal of screens and the cleaning of sills is included. Many-paned or hard-to-reach windows are $1 extra.

Jack arranges for a convenient time and writes the agreed-upon hour in his appointment book and on the back of the card he leaves with his customer.

Let the Sun Shine In is busiest around spring-cleaning time, the end of summer, and before the Christmas holidays.

Jack's Comments: "I think the name of my business contributes to its success. Let the Sun Shine In is friendly-sounding. It leaves the customers with a positive feeling about what my clean-window service can do for them."

PART-TIME PARTS PICKUP

Commercial growers in Bill's rural farming area had to jump into their trucks several times a day and run into town to take care of annoying machinery breakdowns, replacements, or repairs. Then Bill took over that time-consuming chore. And now, as he picks up parts, he picks up a dependable income as well.

Advertising: Word of mouth.

Initial Supplies: Pickup truck, notebook.

Method of Operation: The success of Bill's service depends on how quickly he responds to a breakdown call. "If a farmer has to spend valuable time trying to get hold of me, he might as well run into town himself," he says. So Bill gives each farmer a list of his other accounts along with his home phone number. His mother is usually available to take messages. Bill checks home frequently and also lets his clients know where he is headed next. "Breakdowns don't happen by appointment," he says. "I may be needed again when I'm only half a mile down the road."

Bill keeps a journal for each of his accounts. As he makes his rounds, he notes the date, time, and type of pickup. He sends out bills twice each month.

Bill charges $2 a stop. During the summer he clears $500 a month, the rest of the year about half that amount.

Bill's Comments: "I have a physical disability that impairs my speech and movement. It was discouraging to apply for employment and be turned down. So I decided to be my own boss. Parts pickup is nuisance work for the farmers, but it's a good-paying job for me."

FLYING CLEAN

Whitney washes airplanes. A licensed pilot, Whitney raised her hand when the manager of the flying club she belongs to lamented the task of keeping the planes shined up for each flight. Whitney volunteered to do the job and has been cleaning up ever since.

Advertising: None.

Initial Supplies: A three-wheel motorized scooter, 50-gallon water drum, hose, grease-cutting detergent, sponges, long-handled brushes.

Method of Operation: Whitney found a broken-down scooter in a corner of the airport repair shed and had it put in running condition. She loads her cleaning equipment on the scooter, fills the 50-gallon drum on the back with water, picks up a portable pump owned by the club, and checks with the manager on which planes are to be washed.

"Then I scoot on out to the field and go to work," Whitney says. It takes her twenty minutes to shine up a plane. She is paid $3 to $4, depending on size, for each one. "I have a separate contract with the Highway Patrol to wash their plane once a week for $20 a month," she adds.

Whitney clears about $60 when she washes two afternoons a week for four hours.

Whitney's Comments: "Washing planes is pretty much seasonal work—spring and summer. In winter, the rain does my job for me."

You Can Learn a Skill and Sell It

Your unique know-how can mean money for you.

What do you know how to do? Are you mechanically inclined? Knowledgeable about animals? Artistic? Athletic? Become an expert. Your skill can be your gold mine.

What's more, people who are skillful at doing something generally enjoy performing the task at hand. Based on ability, the business you invent can be a rewarding, far-from-tedious way to put a jingle in your pocket.

All six of the ideas presented here have in common originators who possessed specific skills. Some brainstormed their ideas first and then learned the skill that turned creation into cash. Others inventoried existing skills and matched business to ability. But all proved that when you have a skill, you can sell it.

THE GOOD DEAL WHEEL SHOP

Gene became a bicycle repairman when his father said, "You can buy a ten-speed if you learn how to fix it. I don't want a lot of money spent on repairs."

Gene wanted that ten-speed, so he read manuals, hung around bike shops, and asked a lot of questions. When he could expertly take apart and put together his own bike, Gene set out to repair others. His family garage is now The Good Deal Wheel Shop . . . Inexpensive Bicycle Repair a Specialty.

Advertising: Gene advertises in his neighborhood newspaper's free classified-ad section. When business is slow, he gets on his bike and distributes his business cards door to door.

Initial Supplies: Cluster tools for freewheel removal, tire irons, chain tool, air pump, patch kit, grease, and light oil.

Method of Operation: Gene made up an itemized list of costs based on the time it took to fix routine bicycle ailments: 75 cents to patch an inner tube, 50 cents to put in a new one, $5 for a basic clean-up and lube job. The average repair nets Gene around $2. A complete overhaul, however, can run as much as $15. If parts are needed, Gene buys them and staples the sales slip to the customer's bill. He also supplies used parts at bargain rates.

In its first summer of operation, The Good Deal

Wheel Shop cleared $120 after Gene bought the basic tools needed to set up business.

Gene's Comments: "The only bad thing about bike repair is when you fix a flat and the owner goes for a ride and immediately gets another. There's no way you can convince him you fixed the first flat right. So you patch up the second one for free."

LUG-A-LOG

Lou's Lug-A-Log makes quick work of winter's woodpile-to-fireplace chore. His log carrier is a rectangular piece of canvas with rope handles secured to each end. Lay it out flat, pile on the logs, pick it up by the sturdy handles, and enough wood for the evening is easily brought inside.

Advertising: Most of Lou's sales are made door to door. He presents his card as he asks, "Do you have a fireplace?" Then he shows the sturdiness of his sample, emphasizing the ease of carrying a large load and the way it keeps bits of bark off the rug. He suggests Lug-A-Log as a welcome, practical gift for friends and family.

Two nurseries sell the log carriers on consignment and take 15 percent of Lou's $8.95 asking price. During the holiday season, by arrangement with the owner of a large Christmas-tree lot, he mans a booth filled with his colorful carriers.

Initial Supplies: Canvas, rope, heavy-duty thread and needles, sewing machine.

Method of Operation: Lou can cut four Lug-A-Logs from three yards of 36-inch-wide, 12-ounce army duck at $4 a yard. "The owner of the awning shop, where I buy my material, gives me a 10 percent discount when I buy twelve yards or more," Lou says.

The finished carriers measure 33 inches in length with a 1½-inch hem at each end, by 22 inches in width, with a 3½-inch side turnover. Each corner is turned down into a triangle and securely stitched over a two-foot-long heavy rope handle tucked well down into the triangle. Once Lou figured out the intricacies of operating a sewing machine and made a few log carriers, the cutting and sewing took less than twenty minutes a carrier.

Lug-A-Logs come in warm winter colors of brick red, forest green, and deep brown. Special colors can be ordered on request.

Lou's Comments: "This has been my cold-weather moneymaking project for several years. I've learned there's no use trying to sell Lug-A-Logs in the summer."

AMY'S TRIPLE SERVICE

"Sure you know what you're doing?" That's the question Amy hears over and over again when she offers her automotive service of 1,000-mile change of oil and re-placement of oil and air filters. Amy does know what she's doing and, with a buildup of repeat customers, she efficiently services fifteen cars every Saturday.

Advertising: Amy hands out fliers door to door. "My selling points are cost—they save 40 percent with me; convenience—I work in their driveway, so there's no need to deliver a car to a service station; efficiency—the job is finished in less than thirty minutes; and quality—I use only the best filters and oil."

Initial Supplies: Master Auto Manual, wrenches, oil pan, five-gallon cans for waste oil, oil filters, air filters, oil.

Method of Operation: Amy works only on Saturdays, all day. She schedules appointments at half-hour inter-vals beginning at eight in the morning. Fifteen cars is her maximum work load. When she makes an appoint-ment, she asks the make and model of the car. Then she looks it up in the manual to find out which air and oil filter are needed. The engine size tells her how many quarts of oil to bring along. Fridays, after school, she visits an automotive discount store and buys her sup-plies.

"It's simple to change filters," Amy says. "I learned how in a basic auto-mechanics class at school. I took the class because my father said, 'If you're going to be driv-ing a car, I don't want you stranded if something goes wrong.' Actually, mechanical things come easy to me."

Changing oil is also simple, but messy. Amy drains it into her pan and pours it into the five-gallon can she brings with her. Finally, she refills the engine reservoir with new oil.

"Service stations charge $20 for what I do. I charge $12. On the average, the filters and oil cost me $9, so I clear $3 on each car. That's $45 on a good Saturday."

At the end of each job, Amy asks for an estimate of how many miles the car is driven each week. Then she either makes an appointment for the next 1,000-mile servicing or makes a note to call the customer.

On her way home, Amy stops to sell her waste oil to a nurseryman, who uses it for weed killer. He pays her 10 cents a gallon and supplies her with empty cans for the next Saturday.

Amy's Comments: "People are surprised that a girl would want to do such dirty work. But girls' hands are no harder to clean than guys'."

IVY SCULPTURE FOR YOUR GARDEN

Jim grows animals in a cage, but it's not what you think. His animals are shaped from wire, stuffed with sphagnum moss, and planted with ivy. Jim's ivy sculptures are in great demand as decorative outdoor ornaments.

Advertising: Jim visited nurseries, florists' shops, and decorators' studios. He brought along a rabbit in full leaf and photographs of other animals he had made.

Initial Supplies: No. 9 and No. 22 gauge galvanized wire, wire cutters, adhesive tape, sphagnum moss, flats of small leaf ivy.

Method of Operation: Jim bends heavy-gauge wire into the shape he wants, covering each juncture with adhesive tape while he experiments with the design. He finally secures each cross place with a twist of lighter wire. Then he reinforces the construction by running strands of heavy wire at right angles to the basic design. For further strength (ivy animals are heavy), he wraps the entire frame with light wire. The wire sculpture is then stuffed tight with damp sphagnum moss and planted with plugs of ivy. At this point, Jim's animal looks slightly moth-eaten, but as the ivy grows, bare spots fill in. As a final touch, Jim ties on a small folder detailing the care and feeding of an ivy animal.

It takes Jim the better part of an afternoon to create, for instance, a three-foot-long snail. His cost is $10.

Jim sells his sculptures to nurseries, florists, and, by special order, to decorators. His charge depends on the size and intricacy of the design, but averages $50 an animal. He makes one each weekend and clears better than $200 a month.

Jim's Comments: "I wish people would stop ordering snails . . . I bet I've made a dozen. I try to talk up squirrels, butterflies, anything. But for some reason, people really go for snails."

GOOD DOG

Fido, untrained, is less than man's best friend. But many dog owners are unwilling to spend the time it takes to turn their obstreperous puppies into obedient pets. So Betsy does the job for them. In ten to twelve meetings, Fido learns to go for a walk without straining at his leash, to sit, come, stay, and stop barking on command. For good measure, Betsy throws in a few hand-shaking and roll-over tricks so Fido can show off when company comes.

Advertising: Betsy distributes Good Dog fliers and business cards to pet-store owners and veterinarians. She asks that they please post them in a prominent spot. Her fliers emphasize her dog-training experience. "I guarantee success in the five basics," says Betsy. "Sit, heel, stay, come, and quiet."

Initial Supplies: None.

Method of Operation: Betsy trained her own dog at a city-sponsored obedience class. "I really enjoyed it," she says. "My dog and I became close friends." From that experience, she trained her grandfather's dog and a neighbor's St. Bernard. "With the St. Bernard it was a toss-up as to who was learning obedience," Betsy says, "the 185-pound dog or 103-pound me."

Betsy read every book her library could supply on the subject. "When I felt competent, I went into business," she says.

Betsy works by appointment. She spends forty-five minutes with each dog five days a week. At the next-to-last session, she asks the owner to observe. "At the last session, I turn over the leash to the owner and watch while he puts his dog through its paces."

Betsy charges $2.50 a session. The owner supplies a choke chain, a short and a long leash. Betsy's average work load is three dogs.

Betsy's Comments: "I feel so proud of each animal on graduation day. But at the same time, it's hard to turn over the leash and say good-bye. I get attached to each one."

THE BIRD BUSINESS

Karen never broods over her business, her business broods for her because Karen raises game birds—pheasants and chukars. And while her feathered friends do the laying, Karen's nest egg grows.

Advertising: Karen contacted a sport-shooting club in her area. The owner agreed to buy all the birds Karen could raise.

Initial Supplies: Penning materials, automatic feeder and waterer, heating element, feed, one cock chukar, ten chukar hens, one cock pheasant, ten pheasant hens.

Method of Operation: First, Karen wrote to her State

Department of Fish and Game and asked for their free leaflet on rearing game birds. Then she applied for a domesticated game breeder's license and paid the $25 fee.

Karen's brothers knew of a defunct poultry business willing to give away their penning materials for the tearing down. The poultry growers also sold Karen feeders, an automatic waterer, and a heating element for brooding. Cost, $10. With her brothers' help, Karen built pens according to the specifications in the Fish and Game leaflet.

"I bought my birds from another breeder for $3 each," says Karen. With an investment of about $100, she was in business.

That spring, Karen had 97 baby pheasants and 102 chukars incubated, brooded, and growing. In the fall, she sold all 199 to the club for $3.50 each. Karen estimates the cost of raising them at about $1.25 a bird.

Karen's Comments: "The hard part is knowing that I'm rearing my birds to be shot. I try not to think of that."

You Can Strike It Rich with One Big Idea

6

A big idea can be risky—one false move and you can lose your shirt. But carefully planned and diligently worked, an inspired idea can mean big money for you.

A big-idea business can be a quick, in-and-out venture designed to make a lot of money in a short time. Or it can operate on a long-term basis and be so profitable that it could turn into a full-time career.

So go ahead. Be brave. Think big—but think it through. Some of the seven ideas offered here have made thousands of dollars for their originators. Yours can too!

THE DON'T TAKE ANY CO.

Wooden nickels, giant-size Indian-head nickels, made Susan a pretty penny. Her twice-the-size-of-a-dinner-plate, wood-simulated, polyurethane phony money turned out to be in great demand as decorative items to be hung on home and office walls.

Advertising: Susan did lots of legwork. With a sample nickel in hand, she visited all the stores in her community that might find her product salable—variety, hardware, furniture, and department stores, decorators' galleries, card and gift shops. She offered her product on consignment. When her nickel business showed a healthy profit, Susan ventured into the mail-order business with a $200 ad in a national magazine.

Initial Supplies: The mold, made in her high school art class; wood-grained polyurethane; Don't Take Any Co. address stickers for the back of the nickel; cardboard mailing folders for mail orders; antique brown stain.

Method of Operation: Susan modeled her Indian-head nickel in clay and covered it with latex liquid rubber. Peeled away from the clay, it gave her a permanent mold to fill with wood-grained polyurethane. As a finishing touch, Susan rubs her big nickel with an antique brown stain.

The first nickel she made hangs on her bedroom wall. "All of my friends wanted one," she says. "They're easy to make, so I turned out five or six just for the cost of the material, around $1.75." Susan's father encouraged her to show one to the owner of their neighborhood hardware store. He took twelve on consignment. "We

50

decided on a $9.95 price," Susan says. "If they sold, he would take $3.95 and give me $6. They sold!" The Don't Take Any Co. was off and running.

In October, Susan agonized over the $200 needed to place a small ad in the November issue of a national magazine. But it paid off in spectacular holiday sales. Her biggest bonanza was from a business firm that ordered 150 wooden nickels for client gifts. With mail order, unlike selling on consignment, all the profit was hers. Mailing folders cost 75 cents each. Customers paid the postage.

In January, the Don't Take Any Co. phased out of business. Susan had made close to $3,500.

Susan's Comments: "By the end of December, I didn't want to take, give, or see another wooden nickel. But maybe by next fall I'll feel differently. If you see an ad from the Don't Take Any Co., that's me!"

KIDS INC.

When the Great Pumpkin arises from the pumpkin patch on Halloween, chances are he'll choose Kids Inc. for his first appearance, for Kids Inc.'s pumpkin-filled field is a long-established patch in continuous operation by the seven Delfino kids for ten years. Chris, the second son, is the current proprietor.

Advertising: Word of mouth. However, Kids Inc.

operates in the middle of a popular apple-picking area. Families that come to Apple Hill for autumn apples stop off at Kids Inc. to choose their Halloween pumpkin. They tell their friends and come back year after year.

Initial Supplies: Seed, fertilizer, hoe, cleared land.

Method of Operation: "Timing is all-important in the pumpkin business," Chris says. "The fruit takes 120 days to mature. I plant seeds in May to have pumpkins still on the vines in October. The patch looks better if the vines aren't dried and dead."

Until the plants are big enough to smother weeds, hoeing is a regular task. During the summer months, the field is deeply irrigated every two weeks.

No diseases attack pumpkins, but ground squirrels are a constant problem at planting time. "They sneak out of the woods to eat their favorite food—pumpkin seeds, unfortunately," Chris says.

On October weekends, Chris's patch is filled with families picking out the perfect pumpkin. In the two weeks before Halloween, an average of two school buses arrive each weekday loaded with small pumpkin buyers. While he's at school, Chris's mother collects the money for him. Pumpkins sell from 50 cents to $1.50 each, depending on size. Chris counts his profit from his three-acre patch at close to $1,000. Seed costs around $10, fertilizer $25.

Chris's Comments: "Every September I look at that patch filled with thousands of pumpkins and begin to panic. Suppose no one comes? But they always do. I think I could plant ten acres and the patch would still be picked bare."

THE BIG BEAN-BAG BONANZA

Barbara took a big gamble when she borrowed $300 from her parents, added $200 from her own savings, and rented a booth at the state fair. But Barbara believed in the salability of bean-bag chairs—and hers were a real bargain.

In two days, Barbara paid back her father and replenished her bank account. By the end of the summer, her gamble had paid off to the tune of $6,000.

Advertising: Barbara displayed sample chairs in her booth. Customers were encouraged to lounge on them and examine the material and workmanship. Orders were written on the spot, cash on the barrelhead, with a guarantee of delivery in one week. Or a customer could cart home one of the display models if he didn't care to wait.

Initial Supplies: Vinyl, Styrofoam "beans," heavy-duty thread and needles, pattern from a sewing book, sewing machine.

Method of Operation: Barbara's big bean-bag bonanza began when she made herself a chair. "I knew exactly how much construction cost and how much time it took to put one together," she says. "I figured expenses at $13 a chair." Barbara priced her bean-baggers from $25 to $40, depending on chair size and choice of material, underselling her competition by $40. Sixteen different shades of vinyl were offered, and customers could request special color combinations.

Barbara farmed out the sewing, at $2 an hour, to three friends with machines. When she wasn't manning her booth, Barbara picked up materials, bought from a wholesaler listed in the yellow pages, and delivered the finished chairs.

Barbara's Comments: "Probably, I could still be selling chairs. But why press your luck? The fair ended; my booth was gone. The time was right to move on to another big idea."

YOUR HOUSE NUMBER

When Laura's summer job unexpectedly ended, she was caught short of much-needed funds to start college in the fall. Undaunted, she packed her satchel with paint and set off to make her fortune stenciling house numbers on curbs.

Advertising: Laura walks through a prospective neighborhood and leaves a letter at each house. The letter introduces her as a student and gives a pitch for the desirability of easy-to-read house numbers.

Initial Supplies: A set of number stencils, one rectangular stencil, black and white paint.

Method of Operation: The day after leaving her letter, Laura returns to the neighborhood and begins to ring doorbells. "I'm here to paint your house number," she says. About one out of five says, "Yes, please go ahead." And for each "yes," Laura is $2 richer.

First she paints a white rectangle on the curb. Then four-inch-high numbers are stenciled into the white space with black paint. The entire process takes less than five minutes. Laura usually works in the afternoon for four or five hours. She averages $45 a day.

Laura's Comments: "The big enemies of my number-stenciling business are rain and dogs. Rain, because you can't make paint stick on a wet curb. And dogs, because they're doing a great job protecting their property.

"To improve my business, I'm thinking of hiring some friends to distribute my letter. I could pay $2.50 an hour and still come out way ahead. While they're passing out paper, I'll be where the big money is—out on the street painting."

BRANDYWINE ROOFING CO.

Drew knew roofing ("I helped put a roof on my own house"), and Andy had a good head for business. So the two boys pooled their talents and hammered their way into a summer that finished with sky-high profits.

Advertising: Andy and Drew spent $15 on printing and mailing three hundred advertisements. That mailing brought them enough customers to put them in business.

Initial Supplies: Hammers, nails, ladders, shingles.

Method of Operation: On the strength of their signed-up customers, the Brandywine Roofing Co. arranged with a supply yard for enough shingles on credit to take care of their first job. That job paid the bill and put the company in a cash position to buy shingles for the next roof.

Brandywine Roofing Co. gives free estimates. The customer keeps one written copy, and another goes into the company's files.

Andy and Drew's business boomed. "We had so much business, we had to subcontract friends," Andy says. Instead of paying their helpers an hourly wage, the company paid according to the number of shingles laid. "If someone goofed off, we weren't stuck," Drew explains.

Andy's and Drew's Comments: "Brandywine Roofing Co. made a lot of money last summer, but we worked hard. We put in lots of hours up on those roofs."

THE RAINBOW PAINTERS & CO.

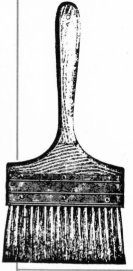

Flushed with the success of his Brandywine Roofing Co., Andy expanded his horizons and founded the Rainbow Painters & Co.—exterior and interior painting of houses. Again he took in a partner, friend Greg.

Advertising: The two boys followed the successful Brandywine Roofing Co. format and mailed several hundred fliers to prospective customers. They made special contact with those who had contracted with Brandywine for roofing jobs. The Rainbow Painters & Co. also placed ads in local newspapers. "But a big sign brings us most of our business," Andy says. "It's a four-foot picture of a rainbow with our telephone numbers on it." The boys put up the sign in front of each house they paint. The rainbow attracts attention, and people stop to ask the boys to drop by their house to give an estimate.

Initial Supplies: Ladders, wire brushes, sandpaper, paintbrushes, rollers, drop cloths, blowtorch.

Method of Operation: The painters give free estimates, breaking down the cost by material and labor. "At first, we figured our time at $3 an hour, but as we became better and faster painters, we raised it to $4," Andy says. The boys work after school, on weekends, and during the summer. At the end of the company's first three months of operation, Greg and Andy's pot of gold amounted to a little better than $1,000 each—and the end of their rainbow is not even in sight.

Andy's Comments: "When I paint a house, I check out the roof. If it needs repair, I suggest the Brandywine Roofing Co. When I'm on the roof, I look for peeling paint and ask if the Rainbow Painters & Co. can give them an estimate. We get them coming and going!"

THE A & P BIKE SHOP

The A & P Landscaping firm and the A & P Bicycle Repair Service paved the way for the A & P Bike Shop. A is Mike Abway and P is Charles Polston. The two boys pulled enough weeds and fixed enough bicycles to bankroll a fully stocked bicycle store, for sales and repairs, a block north of the courthouse in their town.

On opening day, the Chamber of Commerce held a ribbon-cutting ceremony, but it had to take place late in the afternoon. High school, where the boys are juniors, doesn't let out until four o'clock. Business hours for the Bike Shop are 4:30 to 8:30 P.M. weekdays and 9 A.M. to 6 P.M. on Saturdays.

Advertising: Mike and Charles promote their business with ads in their town and school newspapers, business cards, A & P Bike Shop stickers on all bicycles sold or repaired, decorative bank checks, and giveaway bicycle pins. Their shop has also been featured in newspaper stories and on television.

Initial Supplies: Thirteen bicycles, repair-shop equipment, basic business equipment, paper supplies.

Method of Operation: Mike and Charles each invested $2,000 in the Bike Shop, saved from their previous businesses. With that money they bought the stock of a going-out-of-business bicycle repair shop, valued at $1,200, for $340 and ordered an inventory of nearly $4,000 worth of bicycles. "A & P's stock is valued at $5,000," says Mike. "And it's all paid for. We believe in paying as you go."

The boys rent their store for $75 a month. "That is a bargain," says Charles. "But other expenses—utilities, telephone, insurance, business license—all add up." To help cut expenses, the boys rent part of the shop area to a friend, for $20 a month, who contracts to paint bicycles.

The A & P Bike Shop still does repair work. "It's a big moneymaker," says Mike, "especially in the fall when kids are getting their bikes in shape for school."

The partners work together in the store. If one needs time off, the other covers for him. They opened a joint bank account, and both sign business checks.

In their first month of business, A & P Bike Shop cleared $700. "Most of our profits are reinvested into the company," says Mike. "But we allow ourselves a salary of $10 to $25 a week," Charles adds.

Charles's and Mike's Comments: "The most important thing we've learned is if you're going to be a success, you've got to do what you say you will do. If that means missing a football game or something else you want to do, you just have to miss it."

The Right Time and Place Means Dollars for You

7

Quite often a moneymaking idea will come out of the blue and whop you over the head. You'll recognize the whop for what it is when you find yourself saying, "What I need right now is . . ." or, "Why doesn't someone . . ." When that happens, pay attention. It's time to turn your job-inventing imagination on full steam, for there's money to be made selling to the hundreds of people who are muttering the same thoughts as you. There's one difference: while they're muttering, you're going into business.

The five job ideas listed here range from the ingenious to the seemingly obvious. But they all have in common two things: all five business people hear the refrain "Why didn't I think of that?" and all five smile broadly as they tuck that green stuff into their wallets.

GLOCKENSPIEL AND CO.

One October day, Harry rolled a borrowed lab cart covered with a bed sheet into the courtyard of the university medical center located two blocks from his high school. He piled the cart high with thick, Old World–style sandwiches made for him by a neighborhood German baker. In half an hour Harry cleared better than $40. Glockenspiel and Co. was destined to become a lunch-hour gold mine.

Advertising: Harry depends solely on word-of-mouth or, in this case, word-of-taste-bud advertising. Customers tell their friends, and everyone comes back for more.

Initial Supplies: Borrowed lab cart, a variety of wax-paper-wrapped cheese and meat sandwiches, dimes and nickels for making change.

Method of Operation: Harry has a standing order at the bakery for six dozen sandwiches at $7.50 a dozen. They are in a box waiting for him at the bakery when the noon bell goes off in his high school. Within fifteen minutes, Harry sprints to the bakery, picks up the sandwiches, arranges them on the lab cart, and sets up for business in the hospital courtyard. In less than half an hour, all the sandwiches are sold at $1.25 each. Harry then has fifteen minutes left in which to return the cart and gulp down a favorite combination sandwich saved for himself. By the time the noon-recess buzzer sounds again, Harry is back in class—$40 richer.

Harry's Comments: "There was a real need for Glockenspiel and Co. over at the medical center. Students and staff either had to line up in the crowded cafeteria or settle for stale, thin sandwiches from a vending truck in the parking lot. I give them fresh, thick, really good sandwiches that can be eaten on the run."

RANCH SITTING

Kelli and Reese are a dependable team. Together they travel the rural roads near their home taking care of chickens, cows, vegetable gardens, and pasture lands so their neighbors can take a vacation from their chores. "Usually, if people have a cow, they can never go anywhere," Kelli says.

Oh yes, Reese is a horse and Kelli's mode of transportation as she makes her ranch-sitting rounds.

Advertising: Two weeks before summer vacation, Kelli and Reese tuck fliers under the flags on their neighbors' mailboxes. The flier describes Kelli as a responsible worker with 4-H experience in tending animals. "Then, in mid-June, Reese and I deliver 'reminders,'" Kelli says.

Initial Supplies: Horse, notebook.

Method of Operation: A few days before a customer leaves on vacation, Kelli drops by to review what needs to be done. "Most of our customers have three or four acres," says Kelli. "Quite a few raise show horses that need to be put on an exercise wheel. Most grow vegetables and keep small animals." Kelli's 4-H experience stands her in good stead. She once raised a goat that needed to be milked, so milking a cow poses no problem.

"Usually, Reese and I visit each farm twice a day, depending on how often the animals have to be fed," Kelli says. "I tie Reese to a tree while I do the chores."

Kelli charges $2 an hour and keeps a record of the time spent at each place. When a customer returns, she gives him an itemized bill. "Often people say, 'Oh that's not enough,' and give me more," Kelli says. Extra dividends frequently come with ranch sitting. "Usually I get to keep the eggs gathered from the chickens. And last summer some people with an Arabian stallion let me breed Reese for free. She's now with foal."

Kelli's heaviest season is summer, but she also ranch-sits the rest of the year. "On school days, Reese and I get going at 5:30 in the morning in order to make our rounds in time for me to catch the bus."

Kelli's Comments: "Sometimes the work is hard. But when I'm moving irrigation pipes or cleaning a stable, I think of Reese's foal . . . and it's all worth it."

SHOW TIME WINDSHIELD WASHER

Mike's moneymaker came into being when he found himself at a drive-in movie scrubbing away at his windshield with his shirttail. Mike reasoned that if his windshield was dirty, others were too. By the next weekend he was in business.

Advertising: Mike feels no need to advertise his service, but he does use a well-thought-out sales approach based on the idea that you never give a prospective customer an opportunity to get in a quick no.

"Your windshield looks dirty," Mike says. "I'll clean it up for you. Twenty-five cents." He finds that a direct statement of fact along with the cost usually gets him the job. But accepted or turned down, part of Mike's sales pitch is a smile and a courteous "Thank you." He has found that the next time that car comes in, the driver, if treated politely, is likely to say yes.

Initial Supplies: Professional window-cleaning supplies—bucket, cleaner, sponge, squeegee, cloths.

Method of Operation: Mike talked to the manager of the drive-in movie and asked for permission to operate his service. He outlined his plans, emphasizing that he would work only when the show was not in progress, and assured him that he would not harass unwilling customers.

Mike contacts as many drivers as he can before the movie begins and again at intermission. Because cars come and go, he jots down license numbers so he won't hit the same customer twice. He works quickly and always asks when he's finished if the windshield is satisfactorily clean. He washes 75 to 100 windshields in a three-hour night. A hundred windshields net him $25. His cost for supplies averages $1 an evening.

Mike's Comments: "When things get tight at school, I may not find time to work for a week. But then, when I'm desperate for money, I can work every night. I usually try to work at least one Friday or Saturday evening each week. Those nights are the most lucrative. The beauty of this job is its flexibility. The drawback—I sure get sick and tired of seeing the same movie over and over!"

CUSTOM MAIL CATCHER

Mail was all over the place in the large condominium complex where Barry lived. The mailman pushed it through a slot in the garage door, where it fell on the floor. With a few sheets of particle board, Barry was in the custom-mail-catcher business.

Advertising: Barry ran a free classified ad in the condominium newsletter: "Mail Catcher: Made to measure and installed beneath mail slot inside your garage. $2.50."

Initial Supplies: Particle board, nails, sandpaper, stain, saw.

Method of Operation: Barry's mail catcher is a simple rectangular box, stained to match the garage door. In his spare time, he cuts, nails, and finishes the boxes. When a customer calls, it takes only a few minutes to install the catcher. Each box costs 30 cents to make.

Barry's Comments: "At last count, I've sold 135 boxes at $2.50 each and cleared nearly $300. Not bad for a spare, spare-time job."

GINA'S WAXWAGEN WORKS

Gina makes Volkswagens—Volkswagen-shaped candles, that is. Four inches tall, her Waxwagens come in two models, bug and van, and in a variety of authentic colors. Who buys her burnable bugs? Volkswagen dealers, who use them as decoys—"Come on in, look over our cars, and get a free Waxwagen"—and as giveaway bonuses for buying.

Advertising: Gina shows her Waxwagens to Volkswagen dealers in her area. She offers promotional ideas and suggests the slogan, "No other car holds a candle to ours." She takes orders on the spot and leaves a sample candle, along with her business card, with each dealer.

Initial Supplies: Two molds, high-gloss wax, color additive, wicking.

Method of Operation: Each candle costs 25 cents to make. Gina buys her wax in money-saving 50-pound lots and her wick by the 100-yard spool. She found the two three-dimensional car molds, for car and van, at a hobby store and paid $1.50 for each. They can be used over and over again. Gina borrowed an exterior-paint sample chart from a dealer and matches her Waxwagens to actual car colors.

Gina delivers her Waxwagens to the dealers and collects $2 a candle. Total candles sold to date, three hundred. Profit, $425.

Gina's Comments: "Now if I could only find molds for other makes of automobiles, I could have the whole car-candle business sewed up."

Sure-Fire Words That Sell

8

The experts call them power words. They're sure-fire words that sell—words that set off a positive emotional response in your customer toward your product or service.

When you make use of power words, your home-made fudge is not just "good," it's "chocolate velvet." Your firewood does not just land in the fireplace and burn—instead "it burns in winter as only summer-seasoned mountain oak can." Your lawn fertilizing and weed-control service will "punish invasive dandelions and give you a spring-lush lawn." These picture-making power words paint desirable mental images in your customer's mind.

Other power words point out how you can make life easier, less costly, or more pleasant for your potential buyer. "This is what I can do for you." "Reliability."

"Money-saving." "Guaranteed." "Trouble-free." All are sure-fire words that sell.

Still other power words tell your customer that you recognize him as a special individual. "Designed with you in mind." "Lessons that teach what you want to know." "A service for the man with more important things on his mind."

Flattering? Yes. Phony? No. Because to be effective, power words must be true. Your "designed for your living room alone" needlepoint pillow will quickly lose its charm when an identical one turns up on the couch next door. And you'll be in trouble if your "trouble-free" lawn mower repair service doesn't produce a lawn mower that sparks to life at grass-cutting time.

When your power words are written, print them up on colorful paper that suits the service or product you hope to sell, for colors pack an emotional wallop, too. A green flier advertising your gardening service reminds your customer of the neatly trimmed lawn he hopes to have. Blue is a soothing color; beige and brown are low-keyed, respectable, and reliable shades. Red, orange, and gold are exciting, eye-catching colors that can be effectively used together for dramatic impact.

Play up selected power words with underlining, capital letters, or a contrasting shade of ink. And don't forget that the name of your business is a power phrase. Give it star treatment whenever you write it out.

Become aware of how power words affect you. Listen

to TV commercials with a new ear. Make a list of sure-fire words designed by advertising experts to entice you to buy their brand instead of someone else's. Adapt their professional techniques when you describe your product or service. Your success may hinge on your skillful presentation of words.

Remember that while you're delivering your sales pitch, written or spoken, your customer is constantly weighing "yea" or "nay." The crucial time of wavering between yes and no comes after the question, "How much?" Professional salesmen call this crucial time "the closing." It's then that the skillful use of words can tip the scales in your direction.

Never answer "How much?" with "$3 an hour" or "$16.95" and stop dead in your tracks. Instead, take a quick breath and sum up what that money spent will buy. "Three dollars an hour. I'll prune your roses back to the new growth buds, haul the cuttings away, take care of ugly flower-eaters with dormant spray, and your roses will be raring to bloom come spring. Is nine o'clock on Saturday a good time for you?" The sure-fire words and the summing-up can change "Sorry" to "Sold. See you on Saturday."

But whether the answer is yes or no, always end with the short two-word power phrase, "Thank you." A gracious "Thank you" after a turndown may later change to "Thank you, I've enjoyed working for you. Please call me again."

Tips on Advertising

Tim the Weedman ties this attractive card on every bunch of decorative grasses he sells. The unpretentious card, printed in deep brown on straw-colored paper, subtly enhances the product he sells.

Emperor Norton's Imperial Orchestra

Classical Chamber Music for Parties, Weddings & Other Occasions

629-1148   854-4428

Emperor Norton himself might have printed up these discreetly ornate fliers. Placed in easy reaching distance for listeners to pick up, the fliers have resulted in high-paying playing engagements for Rob's group of San Francisco street musicians.

Frugal Leslie makes good use of her senior-year calling cards. The cartooned animal, drawn in brown on the buff-colored cards, dramatizes her name, and although the cards are small, Leslie uses both front and back to advertise her abilities as a commercial artist.

Let the Sun Shine In

WINDOW WASHING BY JACK • FREE ESTIMATES

Sometimes a single picture is worth a thousand words.

Bright yellow construction paper, a smiling sun peering through a sparkling window, and a boy... undoubtedly Jack, the window washer, admiring his work... all add up to a simple, yet effective, business card.

Betsy's mimeographed flier is a cheerful advertisement that reflects her attitude toward her four-legged charges. On the flier, the descriptive name of her business is given appropriate top billing. At the bottom of the sheet, the slogan, "A well-trained dog is a happy dog," effectively implies the power words, "This is what I can do for you and your dog." And what Betsy proposes to do is clearly listed in the center of the advertisement as a five-point program. The drawing of the dog leaves no doubt that this is a portrait of the customer's pet when he has successfully graduated from Betsy's Good Dog school.

Laura's mimeographed letter makes good use of "helpful" power words. First, she outlines what her house number service will do to make life easier for her potential customer. Then she turns her power words around and gives the customer a chance to feel good by helping her. Finally, she ends with a polite "thank you" and finishes off her flier with a clever drawing.

DEAR RESIDENT:

TOMORROW I WILL STOP BY YOUR HOUSE TO OFFER YOU A MUCH NEEDED COMMUNITY SERVICE... YOUR HOUSE NUMBER PAINTED CLEARLY AND DISTINCTLY ON YOUR CURB.

✓ YOUR HOUSE NUMBER WILL BE 4-INCHES TALL, PRINTED IN FLAT BLACK ON A WHITE BACKGROUND.

✓ YOUR HOUSE NUMBER, EASILY READ, ENABLES FIRE AND SHERIFF DEPARTMENTS TO QUICKLY FIND YOUR ADDRESS.

✓ YOUR HOUSE NUMBER, CLEARLY PRINTED, ENABLES FRIENDS AND REPAIRMEN TO EASILY FIND YOUR HOME.

I AM A STUDENT. THE CHARGE FOR YOUR HOUSE NUMBER PAINTED ON YOUR CURB IS $2.00. BY ACCEPTING MY OFFER, YOU WILL NOT ONLY PROVIDE YOURSELF WITH A VALUABLE SERVICE, YOU WILL ALSO HELP A CONSCIENTIOUS STUDENT EARN A FEW DOLLARS DURING HIS SUMMER DAYS. THANK YOU FOR YOUR CONSIDERATION.

SINCERELY,

Laura Firey

0007

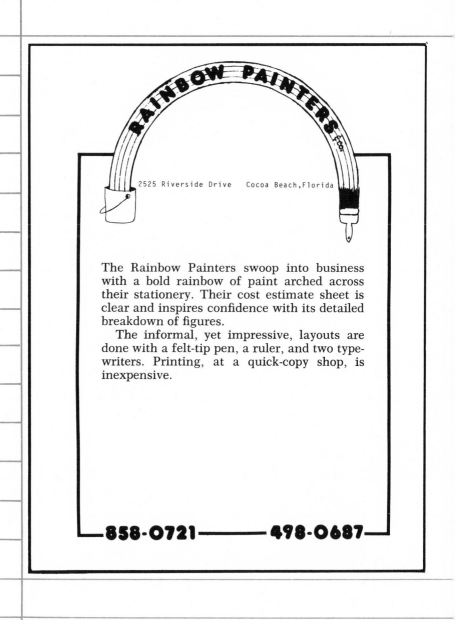

2525 Riverside Drive   Cocoa Beach, Florida

The Rainbow Painters swoop into business with a bold rainbow of paint arched across their stationery. Their cost estimate sheet is clear and inspires confidence with its detailed breakdown of figures.

The informal, yet impressive, layouts are done with a felt-tip pen, a ruler, and two typewriters. Printing, at a quick-copy shop, is inexpensive.

858-0721 —————— 498-0687

ESTIMATE

R.P. & Co.

Type of job:
(✓) residential
( ) Industrial
( ) Commercial

Smith
1000 West Drive

Siding: None

_____ total=_____ sq.ft.

Trim: all upper plus eaves & overhangs

_____ total _____ sq.ft.

Windows: 24 plus bay windows _____ windows

Doors: all (beige) _____ doors

Preparation:
(✓) scraping
(✓) sanding
(✓) 1 coats primer
(✓) 2 coats latex

Misc. materials: "DAP" Caulking (@ 2.15)
wood putty

Paint: 1 gallons @ 400 sq.ft. = 2 gallons @ $12.96 = $25.92

Stain: 1 gallons @ 250 sq.ft. = 3 gallons @ $10.98 = $32.94

TOTAL = 5 gallons = $58.86

Labor: 32 hours @ $4.00 per hour = $128.00 X 2

TOTAL MATERIAL COSTS: $61.01

TOTAL LABOR COSTS: $256.00

TOTAL COST: $317.00

Guy Tipping

858-0721 — 498-0687

The A & P Bike Shop promotes itself like a long established business. From the bicycle imprinted on its bank checks to the snappy newspaper ad announcing the Grand Opening, A & P Bicycle Sales & Service comes across as a reliable, reputable place to do business.

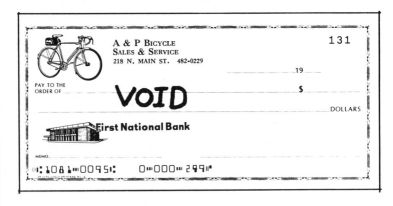

Kelli's flier is duplicated on grass-green, good-quality paper. Her cartoon-style layout light-heartedly frames her clearly worded advertisement for her helpful and reliable Ranch Sitting service.